The Sun Shines Everywhere

Katie Peters

GRL Consultants,
Diane Craig and Monica Marx,
Certified Literacy Specialists

Lerner Publications ◆ Minneapolis

Note from a GRL Consultant
This Pull Ahead leveled book has been carefully designed for beginning readers. A team of guided reading literacy experts has reviewed and leveled the book to ensure readers pull ahead and experience success.

Copyright © 2020 by Lerner Publishing Group, Inc.

All rights reserved. International copyright secured. No part of this book may be reproduced, stored in a retrieval system, or transmitted in any form or by any means—electronic, mechanical, photocopying, recording, or otherwise—without the prior written permission of Lerner Publishing Group, Inc., except for the inclusion of brief quotations in an acknowledged review.

Lerner Publications Company
A division of Lerner Publishing Group, Inc.
241 First Avenue North
Minneapolis, MN 55401 USA

For reading levels and more information, look up this title at www.lernerbooks.com.

Main body text set in Memphis Pro 24/39
Typeface provided by Linotype.

Photo Acknowledgments
The images in this book are used with the permission of: © iStockphoto, pp. 3, 4–5, 6–7, 8–9, 10 11, 14–15, 16 (top left), 16 (top middle), 16 (bottom left), 16 (bottom middle), 16 (bottom right); © Shutterstock, pp. 12–13, 16 (top right).

Front cover: © Shutterstock

Library of Congress Cataloging-in-Publication Data

Names: Peters, Katie, author.
Title: The sun shines everywhere / Katie Peters.
Description: Minneapolis : Lerner Publications, [2019] | Series: Let's look at weather (Pull Ahead readers (nonfiction)) | Audience: Ages 4–7. | Audience: K to grade 3. | Includes index.
Identifiers: LCCN 2018057826 (print) | LCCN 2019005651 (ebook) | ISBN 9781541562561 (eb pdf) | ISBN 9781541558373 (lb : alk. paper) | ISBN 9781541573253 (pb : alk. paper)
Subjects: LCSH: Sunshine—Juvenile literature. | Weather—Juvenile literature. | Sun—Juvenile literature.
Classification: LCC QC911.2 (ebook) | LCC QC911.2 .P48 2019 (print) | DDC 551.5/271—dc23

LC record available at https://lccn.loc.gov/2018057826

Manufactured in the United States of America
2-51156-46218-6/8/2021

Contents

The Sun Shines
 Everywhere 4

Did You See It? 16

Index....................16

The Sun Shines Everywhere

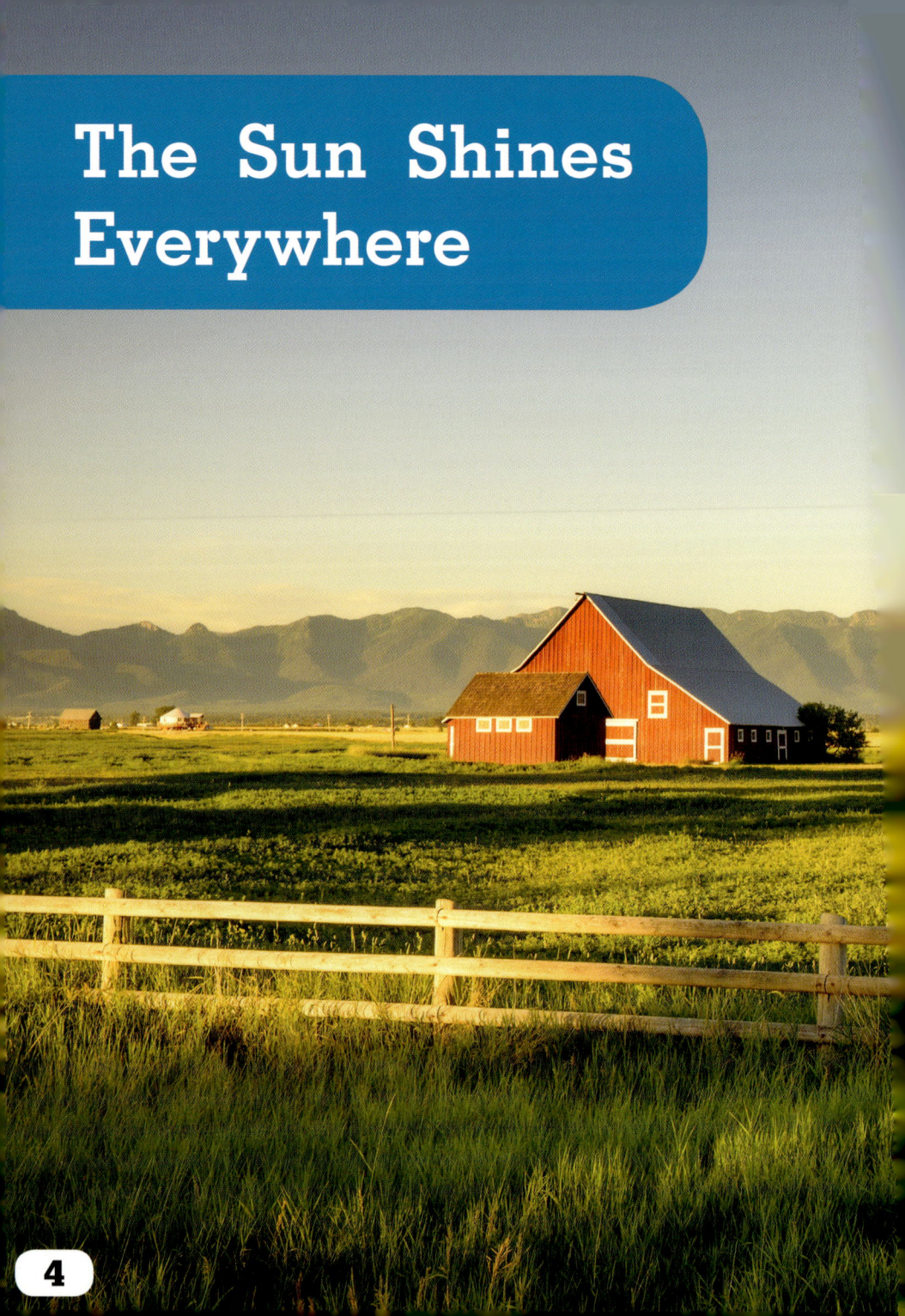

The sun shines on the farm.

The sun shines on the road.

The sun shines on the city.

The sun shines on the park.

The sun shines on the house.

The sun shines in the sky.

Did You See It?

city

farm

house

park

road

sky

Index

city, 9

farm, 5

house, 13

park, 11

road, 7

sky, 15

16